Taming Your New Refrigerator

The Book That Should've Come With Your Refrigerator!

Mike Dobos

Bloomington, IN   Milton Keynes, UK
authorHOUSE®

AuthorHouse™
1663 Liberty Drive, Suite 200
Bloomington, IN 47403
www.authorhouse.com
Phone: 1-800-839-8640

AuthorHouse™ UK Ltd.
500 Avebury Boulevard
Central Milton Keynes, MK9 2BE
www.authorhouse.co.uk
Phone: 08001974150

First published by AuthorHouse   8/8/2007

ISBN: 978-1-4259-5687-5 (e)
ISBN: 978-1-4259-5686-8 (sc)

Library of Congress Control Number: 2006909310

Printed in the United States of America
Bloomington, Indiana

This book is printed on acid-free paper.

Introduction

"Why wasn't that in the owner's manual?" "There should be a book about this stuff?" "What did we do wrong?" These are questions I hear every day. The purpose of this booklet is to help <u>you</u>, the new refrigerator-buyer, avoid mistakes I see every day. It will also help you avoid unnecessary service calls. I run service calls nearly every day which would not need to be run if the customer were better-informed. You will find out the number one cause of first-year service calls, How to handle "no-cool" situations and learn a little bit about how a refrigerator works. I have been fixing refrigerators for over twenty years yet continue to see the same sort of mistakes in buying, installing and caring for refrigerators. This booklet will help you avoid them. This is not a how-to-fix-it book. In fact, though some refrigerators are much like they have been for 30 years or more repairing some newer ones require more knowledge and skill than the typical owner has. Furthermore the typical owner is not really interested in how to fix it as much as avoiding trouble to begin with. This booklet is geared more for that type of owner. I have divided it into 2 parts. Part 1 should be read before you make your purchase. Part 2 should be read soon after the refrigerator is bought. Because I am not all-knowing I can't be responsible for omissions (there is a lot of technical information deliberately left out). Because I am not infallible I can not be responsible for errors (I have tried to avoid them and be as accurate as possible). I have had many customers say that someone should write a book about refrigerator care. This is my humble attempt at such a book.

PART ONE

Preparing The House

Proper care of your refrigerator begins before you buy it. You must be sure the place you are putting it is suitable for a modern refrigerator. Even newer houses can have less-than-ideal places for the refrigerator. Some questions you must ask are, "Will it fit?","Can I get it from outside the house to the place I want to put it?""What are the electrical requirements?" and "Will the icemaker water tubing hook up O.K.?" Walls, floors, doors, cabinets, refrigerators and even people have been damaged trying to fit a refrigerator into its place. It can be a real challenge installing a large refrigerator. Often doors, handles and water tubing must be removed. One must be sure that all parts are put back on correctly. Make sure that doors open and close properly, handles are on tight and there are no water leaks.

Sometimes after doing every thing possible a refrigerator must be returned and a smaller one purchased. One common reason for a "no fit" is the fact that the sides are not usually perfectly straight. They usually bow out slightly (about 1/8 inch) on each side at the center of the panel. This makes a nominal 30" wide refrigerator become 30 1/4" wide. If a carpenter has made the opening 30" wide either the cabinet or the counter top or the refrigerator will be damaged trying to install it. The refrigerator can be scratched dented or warped. Excessive warping can make door alignment and closing impossible. I have seen cabinets hastily cut to accommodate a new refrigerator. It is important to plan ahead either in kitchen design or product purchase.

A fit that is too tight will also make it difficult to move the unit out for cleaning and service. Some refrigerators require space around them for proper air circulation. Rear, side, and top clearance are needed for some units. Others can actually be totally closed in. Requirements are usually in owner's manual but you may not get to read it until you actually have refrigerator installed. Know before you buy. Ask the salesperson to see the manual. A wall beside the refrigerator can prevent doors from opening fully. This can interfere with drawer opening and make some features less convenient. Floors need to be sturdy and pretty level. This is usually not a problem in newer houses. I have seen floors actually be rotted from a slow water leak that went undetected. This can happen if the refrigerator is too hard to pull out for a regular cleaning. Older houses that have settled unevenly can cause leveling problems. Often only the front feet or rollers are adjustable on the refrigerator. Thin boards or shims may be needed to get unit to be level. If unit is not level, or close to it, doors may not line up right and cabinet may be twisted. Severely sloped installations can cause poor defrost drainage and weird-looking gelatin desserts.

If your floor can tear or be scratched easily be sure to have a way figured out to prevent damage before you need to move the refrigerator. YOU may be the one who has to move it. Some companies have damage waivers to sign before they will move it if there are concerns about floor damage. This is becoming more common as refrigerators get heavier and soft vinyl and hardwood floors become more popular. If something important falls behind refrigerator you will be the one to move it. If you need to move it for regular cleaning **you** will need to move it. Thin pieces of panel or hardboard sheets can be used to shield floor from weight. There is getting to be more and more emphasis on '"owner responsibility" While delivery people may put the unit in your house the details of good installation may be up to you. There is one company in my area that will not even bring refrigerator into the house. Avoid this type of company.

Many modern refrigerators have icemakers and water dispensers. These have kept me employed more than any other feature. Poor water supply to the refrigerator is the most common reason for service calls on units less than one year old. I receive a "no ice" or "no water" service call. I get there and find nothing wrong with refrigerator. What I find is a waterline with poor water flow. Self-piercing saddle valves that have plugged are a common problem. Some water filtration systems can also reduce water flow to substandard levels. Some refrigerator manufacturers recommend that their units NOT be hooked up to reverse osmosis systems. With more and more emphasis on "owner responsibility" repair companies will insist that their technicians charge for calls where there is nothing wrong with refrigerator.

Many newer homes and some remodeled older ones are using regular "hard-plumbed" valves. These are more expensive (you may need a plumber) but usually give years of trouble-free service. In some states they are the only kind that meet building codes.

Another concern about the valve is that it be accessible. Even new construction is not immune to putting a finished wall or ceiling between you and the shut-off valve to your refrigerator. This is at best inconvenient (you must turn house water off to service refrigerator water system) at worst it is disastrous (if refrigerator should leak water to entire house must be shut off until problem is fixed). It also makes it impossible to easily check it for being plugged. Many newer houses are being built with the valve behind the refrigerator. This works real well as long as refrigerator can be pulled out easily and far enough to get to valve. If it is put in too tightly then it is no longer convenient. Sometimes the prefabricated nook that holds the valve is not situated to prevent kinking of water tube. Look it over BEFORE installing refrigerator if there is any doubt be sure to double-check line for kinking. I have included a diagram to help visualize this. A leak behind the refrigerator can go unnoticed long enough for massive water damage to occur.

The connecting tube material can cause arguments; some manufacturers specify copper, others do not; some plumbers prefer plastic, others prefer copper. Stainless steel braided lines are becoming more common. I have seen all three materials; I am not sure any of them is enough better in all ways to recommend one. Be sure to follow manufacturer's advice if there is a preference. Also be sure to know if building code specifies one material over another. From my viewpoint as long as the tube can't be smashed, kinked, or caused to leak it will probably work well enough.

Electrical requirements have become just that, REQUIREMENTS. The days of getting by with two or three other items on same circuit are rapidly disappearing. Some repair companies feel that improper electrical supply is abuse and that it voids warranty. Many refrigerators have several electronic parts that are sensitive to voltage spikes and static electricity just like some computers. The reason for this is they ARE computers. Many units have a mother board that actually controls all functions. Non-grounded outlets or additional heavy current-using devices can cause failure of the electronic components. Defrost systems, ice and water dispensers, temperature controls and icemakers are frequently computer-controlled. Electronic controls will continue to become more common. A newer refrigerator may not work properly in the same conditions where the old one worked adequately. Some manufacturers do not recommend surge protectors- be sure to know the owner's manual recommendation before using one with the refrigerator. If your manual says "3 prong, grounded, properly polarized outlet" be sure that is what you have. This is usually not a problem with newer houses. If your house has been the victim of a low-budget remodel job or was built before the days of 3-prong, grounded, polarized outlets be sure to correct the situation before installing refrigerator.

One installation difficulty that is becoming more common concerns large upright freezers in cold garages. Many of these are automatic defrosting units. The problem is the drains sometimes freeze up and then water does not flow through the drain anymore. The water then flows wherever it can and freezes. Sometimes it can build up enough to block air passages and cause poor cooling. I am not sure what, if anything, can be done in these cases. If you have one of those units just be aware that this problem can occur.

It should not be necessary to remind you to be sure the outlet is live. But…every year I get a couple of calls for refrigerators that won't turn on. When I arrive I discover there is no power to the outlet. The customer has to pay for a service call as well as deal with the fact they replaced a perfectly good refrigerator.

The house must be prepared for a modern refrigerator. Even new houses can have physical layout space or plumbing issues. Older houses may need electrical upgrades as well. A new refrigerator is a big investment. A little knowledge and planning will help you get the most of it.

Buying The Refrigerator

Now that the house is ready it is time to buy. There are several on-line sources that compare brand to brand for quality, price, and reliability. I am not going to duplicate them. I will refer to some features and make suggestions. Unless you have already decided exactly what you want and where you wish to buy I suggest going to three different sources. Most retailers match prices of "similar" items (Remember <u>they</u> define "similar"). You can compare features of several brands. You may even discover features you did not know about. This allows you to compare features brand-for-brand as well as comparing control layout. The trend right now is controls in front where they are easy to adjust. I am not sure it is best. You do not adjust controls very often and sometimes curious children turn controls off. I have had to charge customers for turning a unit back on (another "customer responsibility" item). It is hard to believe a person does not check so obvious a possibility but sometimes they don't. Freezers located near entertainment areas sometimes get unplugged to plug in one video game gizmo or another. Children do not always remember to plug them back in.

Be sure service is available, preferably from the company you buy it from. The trend right now is for stores to set service up with a separate company. This is O.K. as long as service is timely, accurate and economical (see warranties below).

There are "scratch and dent" outlet stores or "surplus" outlet stores which offer refrigerators (and other stuff) for sale at greatly reduced prices. It is possible to get a good deal from these types of stores It is also possible to get a very bad deal. Most of the time merchandise is sold at these places because something is not up to quality standards. Sometimes it is a minor issue. Sometimes it is more major than anybody knows. Before you buy from one of these remember:

1. Know current retail prices-sometimes item can be bought on sale for less.

2. Model and serial number tags are usually removed.

3. Removing tags usually voids any factory warranty.

4. Obtaining correct parts can be difficult without correct model number; it may be impossible to get correct part numbers for drawers and shelves.

5. If unit has a recall you will neither know about nor be able to get it done.

6. Products are rarely warranted by seller.

7. Severely damaged cabinets may have damaged refrigerant tubing.

8. Proper door closing may be impossible with a damaged cabinet.

9. If you can't plug unit in to test it do not buy it.

10. You may have to deliver unit yourself and get rid of old one

11. Be sure all parts are there. Replacing missing or damaged drawers and shelves may be expensive. If you have a good laptop computer you may be able to find out prices of the missing parts right then and there.

12. Cost effectiveness: are the savings enough to justify a long drive transporting it and getting rid of old unit?

13. It is possible to get a very good deal if you do your homework and are willing to bear some of the burden

14. Do not be frightened by "It may not be here tomorrow" statements. The complete statement is "It may not be here tomorrow but something else will be"

I recommend buying where there are knowledgeable salespeople, factory warranty and service after the sale.

Do not let price and features be your only concerns. There is a wide range of construction quality. Be sure to check these four areas:

1. Hinges and doors: Some doors are obviously weaker than others. The same is true for hinges. I have given estimates on 3 or 4 year-old refrigerators for door replacement that exceed cost of new refrigerators.

2. Drawers: These must work smoothly and be strong enough to handle normal loads. Binding drawers = future breakage.

3: If they wobble easily or seem weak they may not hold up in the real world

4. Cabinet: All cabinets bend when pushed sideways-try to find one that bends least

I have seen many otherwise good refrigerators be worthless because drawers, hinges, doors, and cabinets could not be economically repaired.

Cooling systems usually hold up pretty well in all brands. Some are better than others but which is best seems to vary from time-to-time. Know the store's return policy. Also know what reasons for return are acceptable to them if you are not satisfied with your purchase.

Be sure to save receipts and know where you put them. Some warranties apply only for the original purchaser. If your warranty is one of those you may need to prove to the service provider that you are the original purchaser.

Opinions are divided over sending in purchase registrations. Most of the time they are not needed to obtain warranty service. They do help in the event of safety recalls or warranty modifications. You will sometimes end up on a mailing list for "other valuable products" (ranging from worthless to something really useful) if you turn the form in. My belief is they are more of a help than a problem, especially as proof of purchase before a warranty repair. Having the product registered can make warranty repairs have less hassle.

Warranties

Another consideration is warranties. There are several ways to classify warranties (no, not "worth little" and "worth nothing"). You need to be aware of what warranties are available, which ones come with purchase and which you have to buy. Although there are similarities, and in some cases duplication, there are also differences, even by the same manufacturer. One way of looking at warranties is "expressed" vs. "implied". "Expressed" is what is actually written somewhere. "Implied" is a somewhat vague term with some legal implications. It can usually be summed up by "The refrigerator will work if properly installed in a "normal" environment." or "The refrigerator will do the job that it is intended to do". What is also implied is there are limitations on what it can do (more about limitations later). These are not always mentioned in owner's manual. The usual use of the word "warranty" is related to what is actually written down. Manufacturer's warranty and extended warranty (protection agreement, repair agreement, service contract, or whatever the current name is for an additional warranty you <u>purchase</u>) will be the focus of our discussion. Sometimes the seller also has a warranty usually in the form of a "satisfaction guaranteed" phrase.

Manufacturer's warranty usually has a phrase like "defects in material and workmanship" included. There is also a time frame involved. The tendency of manufacturers right now is that 1 year means 1 year, not 13 months. Sometimes the retailer will stand by the merchandise even though it is beyond the manufacturer's warranty and there is no extended warranty. This is one more reason to be careful when buying from "sale barn" type establishments. Most manufacturers at this time (2005) offer 1 year on entire refrigerator but 5 years on "sealed system" or "fluid system" or "refrigerant-carrying components". In 2006 some sellers and manufacturers will be offering just one year on sealed system components-check before you buy. Food loss is also covered on some freezers. Find out about these things before you buy. It is important to remember that defective materials does not include accidents. Trim and other non-functional parts may also be excluded. Try to read what warranty says before you buy. I have seen warranties that exclude knobs. Evidently there is some secret way to turn controls without them. When I see them broken I usually try to find a way to cover them somehow. Another typical manufacturer's warranty exclusion are "customer instruct". calls. If there is nothing wrong with refrigerator and it is a matter of showing the customer how it works the manufacturer will not pay the service provider for the call. Guess who does. One of the reasons I have written this booklet is to help people to avoid these kinds of calls. Other words and phrases to look for in the warranty are "transportation of unit," "diagnostic fees," "abuse," "neglect," "consequential damage," and "proper installation." To some extent warranties are legal agreements that are subject to interpretation. They are also worded much more precisely than older ones so limitations are more definitely spelled out. By and large though the manufacturer is concerned when a refrigerator honestly is no good. Often they ask for the failed parts to be returned so they can see why. If a manufacturer gets a reputation for producing second-rate products it can hurt sales. Most manufacturers are usually pretty fair about genuine component failure. Some "gray areas" include shelf breakage, drawer breakage, door seal damage (if caused by sticky food or being hit by drawer) and part failure caused by outside factors (rodents, water, temperature extremes, poor water pressure or other things not directly part of refrigerator). Genuine abuse is almost never covered under a manufacturer warranty. Drawers too full, knobs and levers twisted off or overloaded shelves are common causes of part breakage. Problems resulting from installation in a poor environment also will not be covered.

Seller's warranties are also written out. Often more is implied in these warranties than others. The usual form of a seller's warranty that is not purchased is some sort of "satisfaction guaranteed" phrase. Some of these are helpful because current thinking is <u>you</u> are the only person who knows when you are satisfied. Abuse of this type of policy has made some changes coming. The time frame to decide you are not satisfied can be reduced - sometimes to less than the manufacturer's warranty. Also some retailers are getting to be willing to just refund your money and suggest you shop elsewhere.

Additional warranties that you purchase are another type of warranty. Many economists are skeptical of their worth. I have seen many people who were happy that they had them I have also seen many who feel that they were not really worth that much. The value of an extended warranty depends a lot on what <u>you</u> value-not the salesperson and not the home-economy expert.

Additional warranties often fill in gaps of normal warranty coverage Trim parts are often covered for 3 years. Customer instruct service calls are covered by some (but not all; read yours). Periodic cleaning and maintenance is usually covered.

Food loss is frequently covered. There is a trend toward spelling out "customer responsibilities." Very often though the line between customer responsibility and customer instruct is vague. To me it makes good business sense to cover the gray areas rather than argue about them. Often "expendable items" such as filters and light bulbs are not covered under any warranty. Abuse and household plumbing problems typically are not covered. Remember, too, that the technician's job stops where the refrigerator stops. Unless the service company also does plumbing or electrical repairs the technician will not work on anything other than the refrigerator.

If your refrigerator has extra features which are above and beyond a normal refrigerator it is probably a good idea to have an extended warranty. I have seen some "extra" features cost as much as an entire new low-end refrigerator to repair. Electronic components, special drawers, and icemakers can cost well over $200 to repair. Items which have been returned and "reconditioned" may have undiscovered problems. If a lasting repair was not made problems may not show up until after the original warranty has expired. If you got a pretty good deal on one of these it may be a good idea to extend the warranty.

Be sure you know where the warranty work is to be done. Usually it will be done right in your house. Some repair companies will take refrigerator to their shop to do time-consuming repairs. Some manufacturer's warranties do not include "transportation." In these cases you may be charged a fee. Be sure to know before you decide to have repair done.

Warranty coverage ranges from none to very complete. You can control how much by where you buy the product and choosing or not choosing to buy an extended warranty. Find out as much as possible about terms and conditions before you buy.

Delivery

Now that you have picked your refrigerator out you need to decide how you are getting it home. The fate of the old refrigerator is another decision to make. Getting the new refrigerator home without damage is not too difficult as long as it is in original box. You do need to be sure you have enough muscle power and loading equipment to transport and unload safely. Another "customer responsibility" is securing the refrigerator in your truck or trailer. Many places will not help you tie it down so they can avoid responsibility if it is damaged in transit. It is possible to get hurt when loading or unloading as well as damaging house or refrigerator. Unless you are keeping your old one it will have to be moved out of house. Some utility companies will buy your old "energy hog." Check in your area and see if they do. If you have to just "junk it" you must do it in a legal, environmentally sound manner. This can cost more than the delivery and haul-away fee from where you are buying it. This is why most of the time customers are better off paying for delivery and haul-away. If you decide to transport it yourself be sure it is secure in the vehicle. Also be sure to transport it upright. If refrigerator is put on its side for very long oil can migrate out of the compressor. Sometimes it will not go back even after it is upright for a while. Be sure to follow manufacturers' advice when transporting. You avoid a lot of risk by having someone else do the job.

This leads to scheduling and dealing with delivery people. This can be a hassle in itself. Often you will not get a precise time for delivery. Usually you will get a 2 hour or 4 hour "window". Sometimes you will be told "am or pm." Often all the delivery crew does is "deliver" It is then your job to hook up waterline and push unit in place. Other companies offer "normal" installation as part of the delivery process. Guess who defines "normal." If there is not enough room to install without damage or if there is not enough water line to hookup icemaker you may still be left with some installation work to do. If you have prepared your house for the refrigerator you will have less trouble; maybe none.

PART TWO

Getting To Know
Your New Refrigerator

Now it is time to get familiar with your new refrigerator. It won't be cold until tomorrow, you will have to throw out the first few batches of ice and the water dispenser will take a while for water to come out the first time you operate it (the tubing and reservoir will need to fill and air must be bled out).

Many owners' manuals are not "model specific" and may refer to features that your refrigerator is not equipped with. I have actually run service calls for a customer who could not find a non-existent shelf or water filter.

Listen to it as it runs. It may not sound like your previous unit, but as long as it is cooling ok the noise may be normal. Very frequently the <u>absence</u> of sound is the first clue of a cooling problem. A fan which was running but has stopped running no longer makes noise (especially ones in freezers-more about this later). Noise levels which are unacceptably loud may indicate a problem but some units do run louder than others. It sometimes helps to hear the refrigerator run in the store but it won't sound quite the same in your house.

One fan motor to make sure you know when it is supposed to run is the one in the freezer. Most refrigerators still have it run whenever cooling system is running. Some variations from this are a delay shortly after a defrost cycle, a delay shortly after the cooling system starts, variable speed motors, and motors which stop when the door is opened. So what you want to do is open the freezer door while unit is running and listen for fan (these are often loud enough to hear even with door shut). If you do not hear the fan push door switch lever or button and see if it comes on then. Most refrigerators have a fan in the freezer. Some large upright freezers do (others do not), but most chest freezers do not have this sort of fan.

Another common fan is found in the rear and back part of refrigerator. This is called the condenser fan. It cools refrigerant-containing tubing located under the refrigerator. They are usually quieter than the one in the freezer. If this fan fails the refrigerator will not cool. There will be excessive heat build-up. This heat build-up can often be noticed on the center rail of a side-by-side refrigerator. Some warmth there is normal. If it becomes hot to touch there is either a large cooling load or a failed motor. After you have had it a few days feel the rail (if you have a side-by-side). Know how warm it feels normally, then if you notice it is abnormally hot you may detect a cooling loss early enough to avoid food loss. Keep in mind, however that if you have not allowed enough clearance, you may get excessive heat build-up as well. Some "owner responsibility" issues with this fan motor include objects (or small animals!) caught in the blades and hair, dirt, or other stuff on condenser tubing blocking air flow.

Other normal sounds include expansion-contraction noises, water hissing on defrost heater, sucking or gurgling noises shortly after door is closed, ice falling into the ice storage bin, and humming from water valve.

Knowing the sounds you refrigerator makes when it is working right can save food and worry if something acts up. You will know by hearing an abnormal sound that something is wrong.

Open and close the doors. There should be some resistance as you open them but not so much that refrigerator moves. You may hear a whooshing, whistling noise shortly after door is closed. Some units have a vacuum-breaking device to allow air pressures inside and outside refrigerator to equalize; your owner's manual should mention this if your refrigerator has one.

Doors should open and close smoothly with no binding or odd noises. If something strange is heard or felt be sure it is not something in refrigerator or door that is causing it. Bottles stored in door are frequent causes of poor door closing; be sure they will not shift when door is opened or closed. Objects stored on top of the refrigerator can also cause problems. I do not recommend storing items on top, but if you do be sure that they are back far enough so that they do not block the door.

Many refrigerators have special drawers or compartments which keep food slightly below freezing in these fresh food section. These refrigerators come with various names like meat-keeper, deli keeper or convertible drawer. It is important that you know where the controls for these features are and how to set them. For example, if you store vegetables in one of these drawers and the control is set for meat or cheese, the vegetables will freeze and will be ruined. If you call a tech and he determines that this is the problem, you may be charged for a service call as well as having ruined your vegetables.

Be sure your refrigerator doors close completely and seal. This is especially important if your door swing had to be reversed. Occasionally, the doors do not hang at quite the same angle after a door reversal. This results in gaps between the door seal and the cabinet. One tip-off is there may be frost near the door just inside the freezer. This frost is not removed during the defrost cycle. It has nothing to do with the refrigerator being "frost-free" (I hate the term "frost-free." There is no such thing as a "frost-free" refrigerator. There are automatic defrosting and manual defrost refrigerators.) If there are gaps between seal and cabinet they can usually be corrected by adjusting the door hinge or heating the seal to get it to fit better.

Get familiar with your refrigerator. Modern refrigerators last longer than most marriages nowadays. Be familiar with what your owner's manual says but also keep in mind that owner's manual may not be specific to your model.

How Does This Thing Work?

"Why does trouble in the freezer keeps the refrigerator section from working?"

A general knowledge of how refrigerators work will help you get more out of it. It can also help you when dealing with repair people. This is not a "how-to-fix-your refrigerator" lesson. There are some good references that you can use; some on-line and some in bookstores.

Refrigeration is simply moving heat. In most cases we are moving heat from where it is not wanted (inside the refrigerator) to someplace else (outside the refrigerator). Various combinations of a refrigerant pump (or compressor), refrigerant, tubing to contain the refrigerant, fans and switches are used to accomplish this. The compressor pumps refrigerant (currently refrigerant is R-134 in household units) through two sets of tubing. In one set of tubes the refrigerant is forced to evaporate. From your science classes you remember that evaporation is a cooling process. This section of tubes is called the evaporator and is usually in the freezer section. A fan blows air by the evaporator and the air becomes cold. The air then circulates around the food and cools the food. Another way to look at it is the food gives up heat to the air, the air gives up heat to the refrigerant in the evaporator and the refrigerant gives up heat to the air outside the refrigerator. If you feel the air being blown by the fan at the back of the refrigerator you will notice it is slightly warm. This heat is the heat that was removed from the food inside the refrigerator. The sides of most chest freezers will feel warm while they are running. This is the same thing happening; the heat being felt was once inside the freezer. The set of tubes that feels warm is called the <u>condenser</u>. The refrigerant which was earlier forced to evaporate is forced to condense in this part of the system. Forcing the refrigerant to evaporate and condense is done by designing the tubing and compressor to make high pressure to condense the refrigerant and low pressure to make it evaporate. It is actually just an application of high school physics.

Day-to-day Care

I wasn't going to spend much space with use and care. Most of it is in the owner's manual and some care and cleaning procedures vary from one manufacturer to another. But there are a few helpful tips I have given to many customers that you may want to know. Some of you also do not have owner's manuals so this should be helpful.

Most cleaning can be done with mild, general-purpose cleaners. Unless you have a manual that states otherwise, avoid petroleum-based products. Some of them can be harmful to plastic or rubber surfaces. Clear plastic containers may be dulled by both petroleum-based and non-petroleum-based cleaners as well. Read label of product before you use it.

Hard water deposits can be difficult to remove if they are allowed to accumulate. I have had pretty good results with warm or hot vinegar. BE CAREFUL NOT TO BURN YOUR HANDS if you use it. I would not advise using more powerful lime removers because they are usually not recommended to be used where food is prepared. Most are slightly to very toxic if ingested and could possibly get into food if used to clean refrigerator.

There are lots of products which claim to remove and/or eliminate odors in the refrigerator. Baking soda seems to work well enough for odors caused by day to day food storage. It is also useful for cleaning interior surfaces (consult package instructions; avoid shock or light bulb breakage; be careful if there are sharp edges). Odors caused by spoiled food from a no cool situation are hard (sometimes impossible) to eliminate. There are some products available that may help. Some customers have had fair results with an open bowl of coffee grounds placed in air stream after scrubbing sides with baking soda. Usually the smells lessen as the unit gets cold again but sometimes it is not possible to get all the smell gone. Lemon juice can also be helpful. I am not aware of any one item that works on all odor problems. Often finding one that works is trial, error and stubbornness.

Exterior things can also cause bad smells. Mice (or pets) can get caught in fan blades at rear and under refrigerator. Mildew can form in the defrost drain pan. Dirt and hair in the condenser tubes can get pretty foul-smelling. Spray disinfectants are useful for these situations. It is usually best to remove the cause of the smell as well. Be advised that some defrost drain pans are not easily removable. Some can't be removed without lifting refrigerator high enough to remove screws. Others are taped in place with pretty tough tape. Most pans are plastic now. Some of the plastic ones are pretty fragile.

Cleaning the condenser is usually listed as a customer responsibility. Some repair agreements still include the cleaning with a yearly check-up but usually once a year is not enough. Some of the units with the condenser tucked under and to rear can go longer in a relatively clean house, however. You will need to know where you condenser (this is not the same thing as the compressor!) is. Look for tubing under, at rear or behind rear panel. A fan will usually be near all but the type that is mounted to rear of cabinet. These are called "static" condensers and have no fan. If you have a chest freezer you may not see any tubing. The condensers on most chest freezers (and some upright ones, too) is actually located just inside the cabinet exterior (if the sides feel warm when unit is running it is usually because that is where the condenser is). This is why freezers with exterior metal damage should be tested before you buy. If the tubing behind the sheet metal is punctured it will not cool for very long.

I have included some diagrams of basic condenser configurations. Look at them and see which is most like your refrigerator.

Some of the condensers which are located under the refrigerator can be cleaned from the front. A long, narrow, brush can often be used to loosen dust for easy removal. Many hardware stores sell brushes specifically for cleaning refrigerator condensers. Some may only have a small section which can be cleaned with a vacuum. I have had fair results using the blower feature of my vacuum. This can get sloppy unless you have another vacuum to catch dust as you blow it out. My shop vac has one hole for blowing and one for sucking. I just hook a hose to each and it works pretty well. The key is frequent cleaning; then there is not so much dust in air at once. Remember, too, that if you have no provision to move unit you can't clean it regularly.

Door seal care is the subject of much discussion. If you have your owner's manual know what the manufacturer recommends. Some repairmen swear by petroleum jelly; however some manufacturers say not to use petroleum products. I use a citrus oil cleaner to clean and lube the seal. Non-petroleum vinyl protecterants may also work. Silicone grease (not the spray) lube kind also works but it is spendy. My experience has been most door seals do not harden and crack during the normal life of the refrigerator (if your unit lasts longer than normal they may harden, however.) The most common causes of failure are unremoved food getting sticky and

and unplugging it. It may be very hot as well so be sure you prevent being burned. If you see an object caught in fan carefully remove it and see if the fan works. Again, be sure you keep fingers away from moving blade. If it looks like rest of refrigerator is working and fan in back is only problem a household fan can sometimes be used to blow air on compressor and tubing. This is not a fix but it can keep food cool while you wait for a repair technician. Just be sure children and pets can't get hurt. If the fan in the freezer is not working it is time to call a repair tech unless your repair skills are better than average. There are just too many ways on some refrigerators for the fan to not get power to run to just change it without checking things out. Look for excessive frost in rear of freezer compartment. Excessive frost in this area may indicate an automatic defrost system failure. Frost will block air flow. Typically you will notice the <u>refrigerator</u> section not cooling before you notice the freezer section has trouble. I usually check for this early in my troubleshooting and customers often wonder why I am looking there when the freezer seems to be cooling ok. If you see a lot of frost cooling can often be temporarily restored by getting all frost melted. Caution is needed though. Usually there will be more water produced after the frost melts than the drain pan can hold. You must be sure you can contain it all or control where all the water goes. Water damage from a "no cool" can cost more to fix than the refrigerator. There are four main sources of water: 1. melting frost in event of a defrost system failure 2. water from melting ice running through dispenser assembly (on units with ice-through-door dispensers) 3.melting food (may get other liquid such as melted blood or ice cream as well) 4. Melting condensation from inside doors. This will continue to drip hours after unit is fixed. Sometimes not much is there; other times there may be a surprisingly large amount. Watch for all theses water sources and be ready for them. Another source of water is leakage from a poorly installed waterline that is ok until moving refrigerator loosens a fitting or breaks a tube. If this happens to you be sure it is fixed. Be careful if you use heat to melt any frost as plastic parts can melt easily.

Another source of water can occur when an icemaker stops working. Sometimes a water line will have broken or come loose. Any time you have a "no ice" problem it is wise to make sure there is no water leak. The water may flow only when the icemaker is in the part of its cycle when it fills with water. It can be tricky to find.

One service call that is rarely worth running is an out-of-warranty chest freezer that runs and does not cool. These are nearly always sealed system problems and repair will usually exceed replacement cost. Unless you can get a deal where cost of service call is applied to new purchase you are usually money ahead to not call anyone to fix it.

If your refrigerator will not cool and you can't fix it then it is time to call a service technician. While you are waiting for repair you need to minimize damage. There are three types of damage to minimize: 1. Food loss 2.property damage 3. Damage to you

Food loss can be minimized by cooking food that is not spoiled and refreezing it in another freezer. Frozen food that has not thawed can simply be put into another freezer. There may be some loss of taste but it is still safe to eat. Throwing an impromptu block party has been used by some of my customers. Having some fun with the neighbors also helps relieve stress. If you know your neighbors they may also put some of your unspoiled food in their refrigerators. It is a sad commentary on today's society to see that some people are not on good enough terms with their neighbors to ask for help like that.

Property damage is also an issue. As mentioned earlier, melting frost and ice can cause substantial floor damage. If there is a finished ceiling below it can be damaged as well. You must also be sure the water line does not leak if you pull refrigerator out. Floor and cabinet damage can also occur when refrigerator is moved. Be sure if you move it yourself that objects on top do not fall and break or hit and injure you. In rare instances failed parts can cause smoke damage. Also the spoiled food can "damage" the refrigerator by leaving a lingering foul smell. It is best if you can get food out before it smells bad. If you have a repair agreement or warranty which includes food loss you may be required to give some proof of loss. Find out what is acceptable to the warranty provider before a "no cool" occurs (like, when you buy). I prefer to take a customer's word for the loss rather than sort through some spoiled food to figure out how much it was worth.

A "no cool" situation can be a trying time-especially if you have to wait for repair. Another factor to keep in mind is the possibility of food poisoning. No amount of food saved can compensate for a case of food poisoning-if you have any doubt about the safety of what you find throw it out and be safe.

Be careful if you move refrigerator avoid pinched fingers and toes. If you attempt self-repair avoid shock, cuts, burns (some parts stay hot a long time) and frostbite (if you puncture a refrigerant line this is a real possibility). Dangers like these are one reason why I hesitate to advise self-repair.

When a refrigerator does not cool you can try a temporary fix, repair it yourself if you know how or call a repair company. In all cases try to minimize food and property loss and be sure you do not jeopardize your health and safety.

Handling The Service Technician

The first step in handling the service tech is making sure he (or she) can find your house. Houses in new developments are not always on maps; street signs can be missing; construction may close roads. Be sure your house number is very visible and easy to spot. Sometimes the number blends in with the house color; seasonal decorations can obstruct the view-so can new growth from shrubs; snow can also block sight. A house number on a garage door may be easy to read when the door is closed but impossible to read when the door is open. A number on a tree in the yard may be missed if tech is looking only at the house or on a mailbox. Rural roads where a tech is unfamiliar can be confusing. When giving directions try to use names of roads that are on the signs and a few current landmarks. Tech may not know "Where the old school used to be" or "The old highway ABC." If a rural house does not have a 911 street address a good description of the house helps. If call is being done after dark have a light on; some house numbers can not be seen in the dark

Technicians are human-or close to it. They come in a wide variety of temperaments, personalities, skill levels and knowledge levels. Most are qualified to repair the vast majority of refrigerators they see. Keep in mind that most of the time they are not sitting in a shop waiting for calls. They are usually booked full, frequently overbooked, and are not wanting to put in an extra long day. Even so the tech should always take the time to be thorough. A sign I have seen reads "If you don't have time to do the job right the first time when will you have time to do it again?" Repeat jobs cost everyone. A tech can do a routine job fairly quickly and accurately. It may look like a rush job but isn't. A tech who takes longer to do routine jobs may be lacking the experience it takes to do the job quickly. If the end result is a properly working refrigerator all is well. How fast a diagnosis takes is often a matter of troubleshooting routine. Some techs as a personal preference start at different areas. The person who starts where the problem actually is looks brilliant. If he starts at the "wrong" place he may take longer. Sometimes we get lucky and find the problem right away. Other times we check something which turns out to be working ok before we find the trouble spot. What it amounts to is this-if there are four potential problems we can pick the right one first, second, third or fourth. If we pick the right one first we look good. If we pick it fourth we look bad. Occasionally you will get a complete "rookie" to work on your refrigerator. Again, if it works when he is done all is OK as long as you are not charged additionally. If you have doubts about the tech's competency feel free to call the repair company and let somebody know. Keep in mind that if you simply ask the tech to leave your repair may be delayed. (If you are uncomfortable with tech or genuinely doubt the skill do not be afraid to call the office first, then go ahead and ask). Do not threaten the tech with phrases like "I'll have your job" or "I will call my attorney" My response was to make sure they had the needed phone numbers and leave as politely as possible. You should not have to put up with rudeness, but neither should the tech.

Be sure the technician knows the problem that is to be repaired. If it is a "no cool" it is obvious. Other repairs may take communication. I have followed up on techs who left an <u>ice</u> <u>dispenser</u> unrepaired because the work order and the customer said the <u>icemaker</u> was not working He saw a full bin of ice and assumed icemaker was working and problem was fixed. Cases like that one are the result of a tech in a hurry (and not being thorough) and a customer who was not specific enough describing the problem.

Some techs do not mind if you watch and ask questions; others do. I usually do not mind as long as they keep a safe distance from anything that could hurt them and the questions are "honest"- not just looking for ways to squirm out of paying the bill. Often customers appreciate my skill when they see what is involved with making a good repair. Some technicians do not like to be asked "How long have you worked for company XYZ?" or "How long have you been doing this kind of work?" The reason is there is usually a hidden question- "Have you done this kind of work to be qualified?" My usual answer is "Too long!" It is a true answer-just not the one that was expected.

Try to keep children and pets in a safe place. I am usually too accommodating to children and pets but I always watch out for their safety. It is not every day a stranger comes into the kitchen and starts taking the refrigerator apart so children are naturally curious. This curiosity can supersede other needs. I was fixing a furnace once and it became obvious that a child needed a diaper change. His mother asked "Don't you want your diaper changed?" The child responded "No, I want to watch him in my poop!" And he did. Friendly pets can distract a tech. I have actually had parts and tools taken. Unfriendly pets can distract or injure a tech. Some techs will not work near a pet that seems threatening. Also a barking dog can prevent a tech from hearing noises well. A tech actually flat-out left my ex-wife's house when he learned my son had pet snakes.

Offer to turn lights on. The tech will not know where the switches are or if there is a reason the lights are off. Noise level is also an issue with some techs. If the tech needs to hear something it is hard to compete with game shows and talk shows.

You should not tolerate genuine rudeness. If you feel a tech has been rude the supervisor should hear about it in a civilized manner. If rudeness is typical behavior the tech will not last long. If it was a rare flare-up the supervisor still needs to know about it. Sometimes personal lives can affect our behavior on the job. If tech actually threatens violence get out of house and call authorities. Most of the time a person who is a genuine public risk can never get a job like a repairman. There are exceptions and if you find one be safe. If I have a problem with a customer I usually call supervisor myself. That way he is prepared for the call and has heard what I have to say about the incident. The thing to remember is there are some personalities which do not get along together. Once in a while they meet up in the kitchen where there is a broken refrigerator.

If at all possible get an estimate before the repair is completed. Sometimes some diagnostic work will be needed before an estimate can be given, but the tech should have a good idea of what is needed before finishing. The tech should nearly always be able to tell you cost before changing any parts. (Sometimes it is necessary to change a part to see if any other parts have also failed). If parts need to ordered find out how soon the repair will be done and where the parts are being sent. Parts may be sent directly to you rather than a shop or repair company address. Know if you must pay for parts before they are sent (typically, yes).

Taking gratuities is usually against company policy. Most techs have no problem accepting a cup of coffee or a can of soda pop. To some techs (and a lot of managers) this is one step below bribery and is a forbidden practice.

Try to have some idea of what you are willing to pay for repair as well as the payment method. Most of the time payment is expected at time of service. Techs can get in trouble with management if they fail to collect (being suspected of theft is common). If cost is more than you want to pay ask tech how much new unit will cost. Usually the tech will have some idea, but with retailers playing roulette with sale prices it is best to check prices yourself. Usually an estimate will be honored without additional cost for a short period of time to enable you to make a sound decision.

After the call is completed ask the tech what was done and why it corrects problem. See if he found any other problems (Remember it may involve additional cost to fix them).Be sure you understand any warranty on the repair. Find out how soon you will know that refrigerator is actually working properly again.

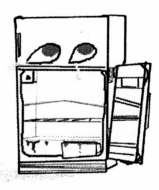

When To Let The Old One Go

One of the most common questions I am asked is, "Is it worth fixing?" This question can be hard to answer. Some of the factors to consider are energy savings, possible future repairs, changes in refrigeration needs and what choice is affordable.

Most refrigerators over 10 years old use substantially more energy than a new one. If this a concern I would recommend not spending over 1/3 of replacement cost on a repair. If the unit is over 11 yrs old 1/4 replacement cost would be my guideline. Some energy usage experts may recommend even less be spent before buying new.

Keep in mind that replacement cost includes more than the cost of the refrigerator. Delivery and haul-away fees are sometimes extra. You also must remember it takes your time to look for and decide what model to buy.

One common problem I see is an icemaker that is expensive to repair. Many of the common repairs to icemakers cost over $200. In these cases one must decide if it is really necessary to have an automatic icemaker. Or, stated differently, "Does it make sense to get rid of a refrigerator that keeps the food ok just because it does not make ice?" Sometimes it does and sometimes it doesn't. Icemakers have become almost standard equipment on refrigerators. In fact there was one line of refrigerator a while back that included the defrost timing controls in the icemaker. The refrigerator would not run without the icemaker. People who brought their icemakers to the repair shop were in for a very unpleasant surprise, when they went back home. I think if the icemaker was one of the reasons you bought a particular model you may want to repair it. If you were not really looking for a model with an icemaker and you think you could get by without it then it may be best to leave it unrepaired. If you do this ask the technician how to be sure no water damage can happen.

Another thing to consider is availability of a suitable replacement. I have been in a few houses where the refrigerator is an obsolete design. The problem is no other current design would work without extensive remodeling. I have seen customers pay for very expensive repairs just because there was no suitable replacement available.

What sort of refrigerator you need can change over time. A household which once had many members may have very few at the time the refrigerator needs repair. If it is not likely that a large refrigerator will be needed it might be time to decline repair and get a smaller model. Some families also get bigger. If a couple is planning on having children the time to buy is before it is really needed. The same is true if other family members are planning to move in. If a change in refrigerator size is likely you do not want to spend very much on a repair. Fixing an older one to keep in the garage for pop and beer is not often a good decision, In the summer it will run more than it did in the house. In the winter, if it gets below freezing drinks may freeze. A refrigerator that is over 15 years old can be very uneconomical. It could cost over $20 a month to keep your drinks cold.

Lack of funds can be a real beast when it comes to deciding whether to buy or repair. I have had cases when a $400 repair is made on one that could be replaced for $600 simply because even $400 was beyond budget. With credit being easy(too easy?) this does not happen as often as it used to. My advice is if your refrigerator is out of warranty start planning for repair or replacement. It may be a few years away but you avoid this sort of bind.

A refrigerator that is under warranty should nearly always be repaired if it can be done in a timely manner. Be sure to keep records of repairs. Some states have "lemon laws" that come in handy in case of excessive repair history. It is well worth your while to check into what your state laws are. One case where I do NOT recommend in warranty repair is when there is excessive repair and it seems that the unit can't be made to work properly. This happens sometimes. The seller may not be willing to replace your refrigerator without legal action. After the 1st in warranty repair you may want to see just what your legal rights are in case of repeated failure.

What Did I Say?

I hope this has been a helpful few minutes of reading. The intent was to make it informative but short enough to read completely before you buy the new refrigerator. The book ended up longer than I thought it would. I still see things happen and say "I should have put that in the book!" Maybe I will have to revise the book someday. I have made effort to not mention brand names. As I mentioned there are publications that do to help you decide what brand and model is best for you. With companies buying companies and companies actually buying some products from competitors what was high quality this year may not be rated so high next year. I tried to shed light on warranties, customer responsibilities, how refrigerators work and how to care for refrigerators. I hope you, the consumer, also got some insight as to how repair people think about refrigerators and the people that own them. I have included some sketches to help show condenser location and cold air flow. They may help you understand the "How does this thing work" chapter as well as the care and cleaning section. Thanks for buying; thanks for reading. I hear my refrigerator running - I have to go catch it.

HELPFUL
DIAGRAMS

FIGURE 1
PREFABRICATED WATER VALVE NOOKS

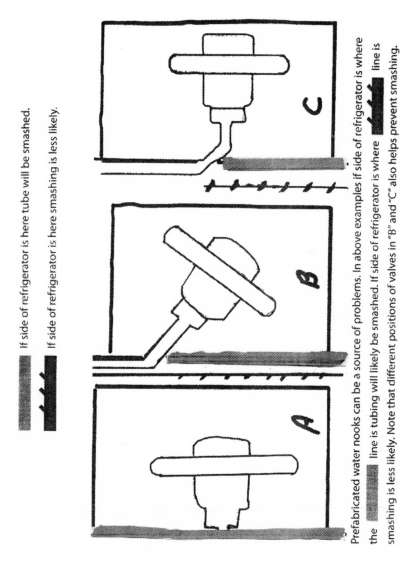

If side of refrigerator is here tube will be smashed.

If side of refrigerator is here smashing is less likely.

Prefabricated water nooks can be a source of problems. In above examples if side of refrigerator is where the ▮ line is tubing will likely be smashed. If side of refrigerator is where ▮ line is smashing is less likely. Note that different positions of valves in "B" and "C" also helps prevent smashing.

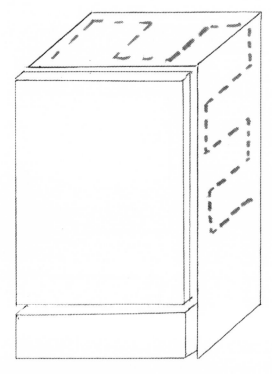

— — — **Represents Condenser Tubing**

Condenser Just Under Outside of Cabinet

Condenser is just under the ouside of cabinet, the design is common on chest freezers and some upright models.

The sides will feel warm, sometimes almost hot, when the compressor is running. It is almost impossible to get this type of condenser too dirty to cool. Poor cooling will result if there is not enough space around it for air to circulate.

FIGURE 3
REAR VIEW OF CONDENSER UNDER UNIT AT REAR

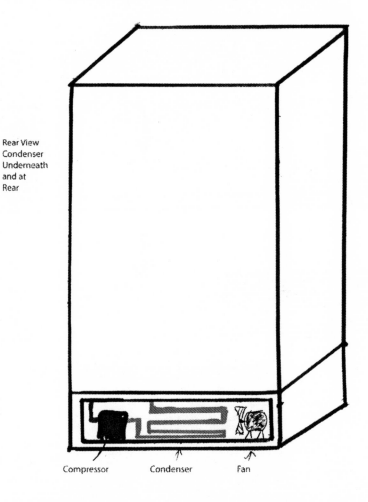

Rear View
Condenser
Underneath
and at
Rear

Compressor   Condenser   Fan

This design depends on the fan blowing air in order to clean it you must pull refrigerator away from the wall and remove the back. Some designs do not cool well with back removed so be sure to put it back.

FIGURE 4

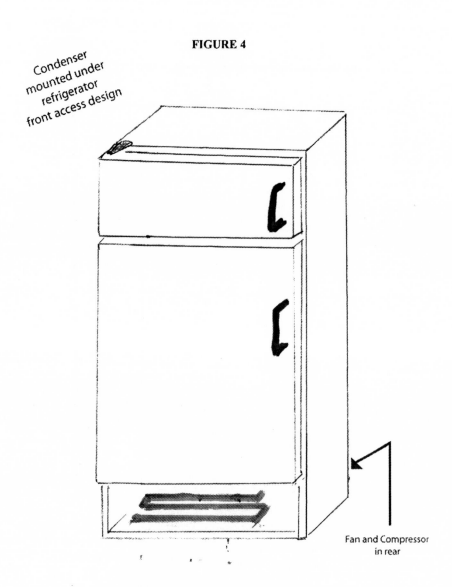

Condenser mounted under refrigerator front access design

Fan and Compressor in rear

This design requires a fan for air circulation.
Clearance requirements vary from model to model.

FIGURE 5
REAR-MOUNTED CONDENSER

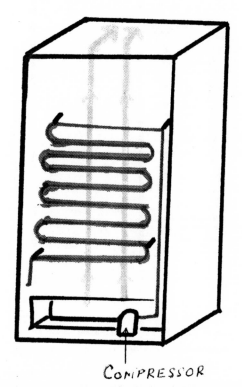

COMPRESSOR

━━━━━ LINE DEPICTS CONDENSER TUBING
ARRANGEMENT FOR REAR-MOUNTED CONDENSER.

━━━━━ LINES INDICATE AIR FLOW.
THIS DESIGN HAS NO FAN. ADEQUATE CLEARANCE
AT REAR, SIDES AND TOP IS REQUIRED. THIS TYPE
OF CONDENSER IS CALLED A "STATIC" CONDENSER.

FIGURE 6
Air Flow in a Side-by-Side Refrigerator

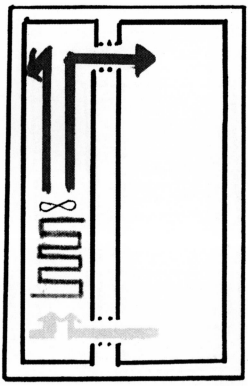

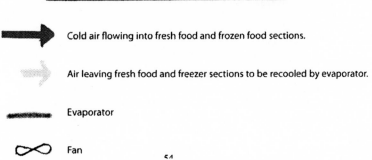

Cold air flowing into fresh food and frozen food sections.

Air leaving fresh food and freezer sections to be recooled by evaporator.

Evaporator

Fan

FIGURE 7

Air Flow in Bottom Freezer

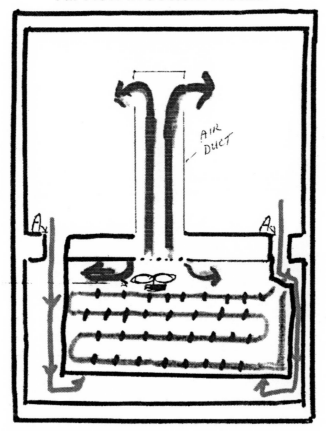

Basic Air Flow of Bottom Freezer

Lines represent cold air being blown into the refrigerator and freezer sections.

Lines represent return air. Return air passages marked "A" are usually under the crisper drawers. They can be blocked if items fall under the drawers.
This will result in poor cooling.

Represents evaporator tubing.

About the Author

Mike Dobos has repaired appliances for over 25 years. He is pictured here giving a 70 year old refrigerator a refresher course. When he is not on the job he can usually be found working on some old item like a car an appliance or his house. He also likes gardening. The refrigerator in the picture is over 70 years old and still gets used when additional refrigerator space is needed like holidays or just after picking vegetables. He lives in Iowa. This is Mike's first book and it is an answer to many customers who have asked, "Why isn't that in the owner's manual?"

LaVergne, TN USA
05 September 2009
157062LV00003B/59/A